Critter County® Power Buddies

Spiritual Boosters for Growing Up Strong

By Paula Bussard / Illustrated by Dan Maurice

Son Power Prayer

Dear Jesus,

Power me up to meet the problems of my day. I really

need your help with _____ .
(name a problem)

Amen.

Critter County® Power Buddies

Spiritual Boosters for Growing Up Strong

Created by: Paula Bussard
Cover and Text Illustrations by: Dan Maurice
Cover and Text Design: Blum Graphic Design
Editors: Charlene Hiebert, Linda Washington
Adventure Series Editor: Marian Oliver

© 1997 Mainstay Church Resources
Published by: Mainstay Church Resources
Printed in the United States of America

Mainstay Church Resources is a new publishing outreach of The Chapel of the Air Ministries. Our goal is to facilitate revival among God's people by helping them develop healthy spiritual habits in nine vital areas that always characterize genuine times of spiritual awakening. To support this goal, Mainstay Church Resources provides practical tools and resources, including the annual 50-Day Spiritual Adventure, the Seasonal Advent Celebration, and the 4-Week Festival of Worship.

CRITTER COUNTY is a registered trademark of Loveland Communications, Inc. Used by permission. Critter County was codeveloped by Paula Bussard and Christine Wyrtzen through their ministry called Loveland Communications. Their books and tapes have been enjoyed by more than a million children across North America. For additional product or concert information, contact:

P. O. Box 7420
Milford, OH 45150-7420
(513) 575-4300
E-mail address: Encouragement @ GoodNews.net

Scripture quotations marked (NIV) are taken from the HOLY BIBLE, NEW INTERNATIONAL VERSION®. Copyright © 1973, 1978, 1984 by International Bible Society. Used by permission of Zondervan Publishing House. All rights reserved.

Scripture quotations marked (ICB) are taken from the *International Children's Bible, New Century Version,* copyright © 1983, 1986, 1988 by Word Publishing, Dallas, Texas 75039. Used by permission.

ISBN 1-57849-042-1

Dear Parent,

You have made a wise and eternally significant decision by involving your family in this 50-Day Spiritual Adventure. You are communicating to your child that regular, focused spiritual study is important to you and to your family's growth as well.

Throughout this Adventure, your child will learn about Son Power, with the help of Critter County friends. There are two new residents of Critter County—Glitter and Sparkle. These Power Buddies will encourage your child to be "energized" by following Jesus. The eight weekly Son Power themes will nurture your child's understanding of the power of prayer, God's Word, and Christian fellowship and instruction. The "energizer" topics are as follows:

1. **Trust God like Jesus did**
2. **Be like Jesus 24/7**
3. **Welcome kids like Jesus does**
4. **Help your leaders as Jesus did**
5. **Pray like Jesus did**
6. **Tell stories about God like Jesus did**
7. **Work with a team like Jesus did**
8. **Celebrate Son Power in your life**

Each week there is a Power Booster memory verse you can work on with your child. To help your child with that process, Christine Wyrtzen has produced an audiotape, *Critter County Power Buddies*, that has all eight verses set to music. You may order a copy from Mainstay Church Resources. (See p. 64.) A complete listing of the Adventure memory verses is found on pages 32 and 33.

There is an activity page for each of the 50 days of the Adventure, plus two warm-up days. Each page includes a puzzle or coloring activity featuring the critters of Critter County. You'll find each week's memory verse and the song title that corresponds to the verse on each page. You will also find two discussion questions and a suggestion for personalizing the Son Power Prayer (p. 2). The questions and written prayers or prayer ideas are intended to encourage interaction between you and your child. There are also two Critter County stories included in this booklet. Unlike the activity pages, these stories have been written for your child to read by himself or herself. Encourage your child to read them aloud with you during those weeks. If you have the *Critter County Power Buddies* audiotape, your child can read the stories along with Christine Wyrtzen's narration.

We hope that you will enjoy the time you spend with your child during this Adventure. It is our desire that your relationship with each other and with God will be richly deepened. So, plan to set aside time to talk and pray with your child each day. Your time investment will have eternal rewards!

His child and your encourager,

Paula Bussard

Paula Bussard

Singing Sydney

[H]ave you met Sydney? He is the leader of Critter County. He and his good friend Christine Wyrtzen like to record music together. Maybe you have heard them sing.

Sydney is a lovable guy who really enjoys making his friends happy. He gets powered up when he helps someone. Can you tell what kind of animal Sydney is? What do you think he has in his snack bag? Does he have potato chips, cookies, or nuts? Whisper what he has to a friend or family member. Then color Sydney's fur brown.

Lovable Lions

O ne of the gr-r-r-eat families in Critter County is the Lion family. Lester is the dad and Liona Lou is the mother. They have one son. His name is Lunchbox. Have you met them before?

Everyone in the Lion family loves to sing, just like Sydney and Christine. Lester plays the guitar and writes new songs about being happy and brave. But sometimes even a big king-of-a-beast like Lester can feel sad or afraid. That's when Liona Lou puts her talents to use. She is ter-r-r-ific at cheering up her friends and family. A smile and a hug from her soon makes a sad lion purr with joy.

Lunchbox knows how to make his friends and family happy too. He reminds us all that being a kid can be a lot of fun even though there are lessons to learn. Color Lunchbox and his family. Give Liona Lou something bright and beautiful to wear.

Power Buddies

Glitter

Sparkle

Y ou probably haven't met the newest animals in Critter County. They are Glitter and Sparkle Firefly. Everyone calls them "Power Buddies" because they light up every place they go. One of the things they enjoy doing most is to shine their lights on the Bible, God's Word. They may be small in size, but they know a great power source when they see it. And they want to help you power up your life with God's truth too.

Sydney Learns to Share

It was a beautiful fall morning in Critter County. Lunchbox and Liona Lou were out gathering leaves. Lunchbox talked about how much he liked Sydney Squirrel. "I think he's a great leader," said Lunchbox. "He's so kind and willing to help people."

"Yes," said Liona Lou. But she remembered a time when Sydney was not like that. Then she told Lunchbox how Sydney learned to care for others.

One sunny day, Sydney woke up early. He wanted to begin his fall nut hunt. He looked in his closet to find his old backpack. He said, "I will work hard today. By nighttime, this will be full of nuts. But first, I will fix some eggs with nuts on top. That will give me plenty of strength to work hard."

After eating, Sydney put on his backpack. Suddenly the phone rang. Kandy Kangaroo was on the phone. She wanted Sydney to come help her start her car. She needed to drive over to the train station. Her cousin was coming to town on the train.

"Sorry. I can't help you," Sydney told her. "I have to gather nuts. Then I will have food to eat this winter. Today is much too nice to spend time fixing a car." Then he said good-bye to Kandy.

Later, as Sydney passed the skunk family's house, he saw Mr. Skunk. Mr. Skunk came outside. "Sydney, how about giving me a hand for a little while? My wife was up all night with our new babies. I'd like to take our children to your house. Then Mrs. Skunk can take a nap."

"No, I am sorry. They would not be welcome today.
I must gather nuts for my winter food," explained Sydney.

"Okay," said Mr. Skunk sadly. "But I sure could use your help."

Many sunny days passed. Sydney's pile of nuts grew bigger and
bigger. "This is the most nuts I have ever gathered," he said
to himself. "But why should I stop now? This pile can be
even larger, if I keep on working."

The critters in the county saw how hard Sydney was working.
But they were sad. Sydney didn't have any time left to spend
with them. All he ever did was gather nuts.

The fall days passed. Soon fluffy snow covered Critter County.
Everyone hurried outside to play. But Sydney could not be found.
"He's surely still out looking for more nuts," his friends said sadly.

But Sydney was not out looking for nuts. He was home sick in bed!
He felt hot, and his tummy really hurt. "I need some help!"
he cried to himself. "I have gathered more nuts than I can count.
But I'm too weak to even fix some nut soup."

Sydney dragged himself to the window and opened it. "Help!"
he cried weakly. "Won't someone please come and help me?"
The playing critters heard Sydney's call for help. They stopped
their fun to talk about what to do. They were all a little mad at him.

"Sydney was too busy to help when I needed him,"
Kandy Kangaroo said. "I had to walk to the train station
to meet my cousin. And then I had to walk home again."

"Yes," said Mr. Skunk. "This all smells pretty bad, if you ask me.
Sydney said my kids weren't welcome in his home. That stinks!"

Everyone had just about decided to go back to playing. Suddenly Cool Cat spoke up. "We need to help Sydney learn what friendship is all about."

"You are right, Cool Cat," Kandy said with a smile. "I will go home and fix him some nut soup." Then the other animals made plans to help Sydney get well. Day after day, Sydney's friends took turns bringing him food.

Finally, Sydney began to feel stronger. "Thank you for taking time to help me," Sydney said. "Your love and care made me get well quickly. My tummy and head feel great today. My heart feels even better. It is filled with love for you. You have taught me something important. Being rich in friends is better than being rich in nuts. Please come to my tree house tonight. I want to share everything I have with you!"

"And I'll bring a special treat for dessert," Liona Lou said. "It's time to party!"

Critters to the Rescue

Lunchbox was happy. He was going on a camping trip with Lester.
Sydney, Glitter, and Sparkle were also going. They were going
to Big Creek Meadow for the weekend. Lester carried the tent
and the poles. Lunchbox brought the food. Sydney led the way.
Sparkle and Glitter used their lights to make the dark path bright.

The hike was long. Lunchbox said, "My paws hurt.
How far is it to Big Creek Meadow?"

"We still have a long way to go," Sydney answered. "But
we can stop to give you a rest. I will put some of the food
in my backpack."

"Thank you, Sydney," Lunchbox said as he rubbed his tired paws.

Sparkle and Glitter settled down beside him. "We wish
we could help you carry the food, Lunchbox," Sparkle said.
"But we're just not big and strong enough."

"You two are powerful in other ways," Lester said. "You light the way for us in these dark woods. If we didn't have your lights, we would get lost in these woods. And that wouldn't be any fun for anyone!"

"Lester is right, guys," Sydney said. "All of us are strong in our own way. This is a great team. I am glad to be the leader."

Soon Lunchbox was ready to walk again. The critters headed down the path once more. Sydney climbed a tree to see how far they had to go. "We're almost there!" he soon called out.

When the meadow came into sight, Lunchbox forgot his sore paws. He dropped his backpack and ran through the tall grass. Glitter and Sparkle tried to keep up with him. Soon Lunchbox was out of sight. Lester and Sydney did not know that Lunchbox was gone. They were too busy setting up camp. Suddenly Glitter and Sparkle flew in. They reported that Lunchbox was missing.

"A lion cub always leaves paw prints," Lester said. "Follow me, and keep your lights shining." Lester was good at tracking lost critters. He led the others to the edge of a large hole.

"Lunchbox!" he roared. "Are you down there?"

"Yes," a small voice called back. "It's cold and dark down here. I'm scared!"

"Lester, get the tent poles," Sydney said. "We can tie them together. Then I will use them to climb down to get Lunchbox. Sparkle and Glitter, I want you to fly down the hole. You can keep Lunchbox company so he won't be afraid."

Everyone helped. Soon Lunchbox was safe at the camp. "Thank you, everyone," Lunchbox said with a happy smile.

"Yes, thank you," Lester said as he hugged his son. "Some critters like to fight each other. But we do not do that in Critter County. I'm glad we learned to work and live together. We can do things better together than we could working alone. It's gr-r-r-eat to have friends like you!"

W elcome to the 50-Day Adventure in Critter County. All the critters are glad to know you will be spending some time with them. But at the moment, they're all out playing hide-and-seek with Lunchbox. Can you find them? Look for Sydney, Lester, Liona Lou, Lunchbox, Sparkle, and Glitter. Circle each critter you find. Then add some other animals to the picture.

The Critter County critters would like to know who's going on the 50-Day Adventure with them. Practice drawing a picture of yourself in the frame that Sydney is holding. Then turn to page 63 and draw a picture you can send to Sydney and his friends. The critters have a special gift for anyone who sends his or her picture!

Day 1 • Sunday

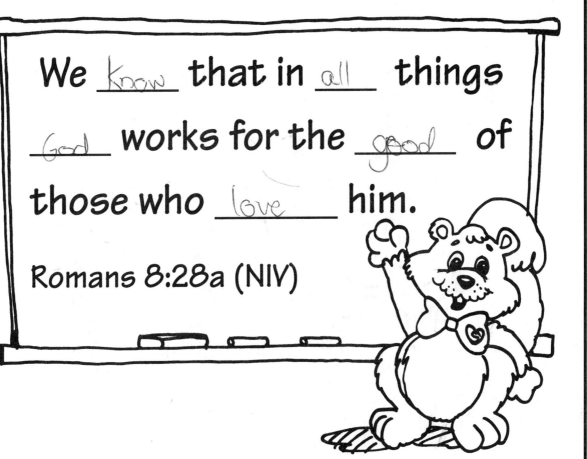

We _know_ that in _all_ things _God_ works for the _good_ of those who _love_ him.

Romans 8:28a (NIV)

S ydney loves this week's memory verse because it reminds him of God's power and love. He wants you to learn and love this verse too. On the blackboard, write the words that are missing in the verse. Then close your eyes and try to say the verse. Sydney says, "Give it a try."

Let's Talk About It:

• How do you feel when you are with somebody who is really strong?

• Can you think of a time when something that seemed bad at first turned out to be good? Did you pray about this problem?

Let's Pray About It:

Pray the Son Power Prayer (p. 2). Remember that you can always trust Jesus. He is always taking good care of you.

Memory Verse: We know that in all things God works for the good of those who love him. Romans 8:28a (NIV)

Day 2 • Monday

P oor Liona Lou is about out of energy. It's late at night and she is trying to make cupcakes for her son, Lunchbox, to take to Cub Scouts. But where is her wooden spoon? Do you see it? Can you color it a bright color so she can find it? Then color the rest of the picture. Be sure to do a gr-r-r-eat job on the cupcakes.

Let's Talk About It:

• Have you ever lost something important? Were you able to find it?

• God can see everything all the time. How does that make you feel?

Let's Pray About It:

Today as you pray the Son Power Prayer (p. 2), remember that Jesus is powerful. He can see everything all over the world. He will never lose sight of you—no matter where you are. He will always be there to help you.

Memory Verse: We know that in all things God works for the good of those who love him. Romans 8:28a (NIV)

Day 3 • Tuesday

O h my! Glitter and Sparkle have just discovered something that looks very frightening. Do you know what they see? It's a giant oyster. Even though it looks scary on the outside, a beautiful and valuable pearl is inside.

How many other oysters can you find in this picture? When you have finished counting them, color the picture. Make the pearl as pretty as you can. Pearls can be white, black, gray, pink, blue, or yellow. What color will you choose?

Let's Talk About It:

• Ask your mom or dad to explain how a pearl is made. Sometimes bad things that happen turn out to be good. How is that like the sand in the pearl of an oyster?

• When you have a problem, who do you go to?

Let's Pray About It:

Do you have a problem to tell Jesus about when you pray the Son Power Prayer (p. 2)? Are you thankful that he wants to work for good in your life?

Memory Verse: We know that in all things God works for the good of those who love him. Romans 8:28a (NIV)

Day 4 • Wednesday

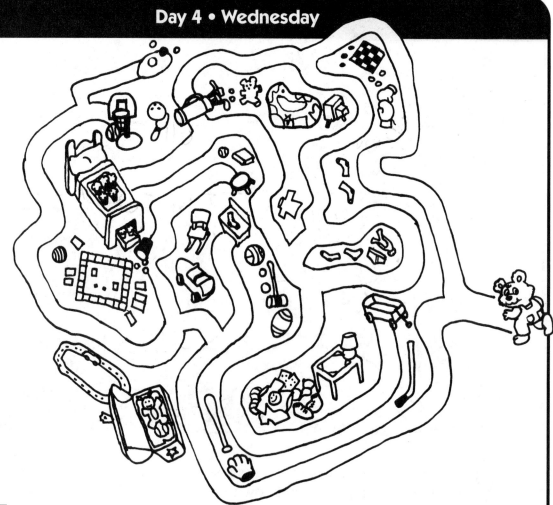

S ometimes it seems like everything is going wrong. Grown-ups sometimes feel that way, and so do kids your age. In fact, Lunchbox has a bit of a problem right now. He has to leave for Cub Scouts in five minutes. But he can't remember where he put the cupcakes his mom baked for him to take along. Can you find them? Draw a line to show him where they are so he can go to a fun party. Hurry, so he won't be late.

Let's Talk About It:

• How can Jesus help us when we feel lost or mixed up?

• Because Jesus is the Son of God, do you think he can see everything? Why or why not?

Let's Pray About It:

Jesus loves to be called our friend. You can call him that when you pray the Son Power Prayer today (p. 2). Don't forget to thank him for always being there. He's ready to help, even when we feel lost or mixed up.

Memory Verse: We know that in all things God works for the good of those who love him. Romans 8:28a (NIV)

Day 5 • Thursday

L ester says, "Now, be careful, my little petunia. You have to guess what this gift is by feeling it. No, it's not a pillow. Feel it again. No, it's not a sweater. Keep on guessing."

It's easy for us to tell what Liona Lou's gift is because we can see it. But she can't. And Lester is only letting her feel the kitten's back. How good are you at guessing things by feeling them? Why don't you cover your eyes and have someone hand you something. Can you guess what it is just by feeling it? Was your guess right?

Let's Talk About It:

• Why is it good to know that Jesus can see in the dark?

• Does knowing that Jesus cares for you make you feel happy and safe at night? Why or why not?

Let's Pray About It:

Jesus can see everything all at the same time. So we don't ever have to be afraid of the dark or anything else. When you pray the Son Power Prayer (p. 2), tell him that you are glad to be his child.

Memory Verse: We know that in all things God works for the good of those who love him. Romans 8:28a (NIV)

Day 6 • Friday

T hese are the doors lots of people tell us we should go through to find happiness. Which one do you think is the right one? God always wants us to choose to follow him and not worry about becoming rich, famous, or powerful.

Draw a star on the door that leads to happiness that can last all our lives. Then color everything except the doors that lead to the kind of happiness that only lasts a little while.

Let's Talk About It:

• Is it true to say that being God's child will keep you from having problems? Why or why not?

• Can you think of a problem that is too big for God to solve? Why not?

Let's Pray About It:

When you pray the Son Power Prayer today, ask Jesus to help you make the right choices. Ask him to help you understand the Bible so you can learn to obey him. That's one of the best choices you can ever make.

Memory Verse: We know that in all things God works for the good of those who love him. Romans 8:28a (NIV)

Days 7 and 8 • Saturday and Sunday

J esus worked hard at everything he did. He didn't do anything halfway. This week's memory verse says that we should work at everything we do the best we can, with all our heart! That's one way we can be like Jesus. He wants us to be like him 24 hours a day, 7 days a week. That means being like Jesus all the time!

Look at all of our Critter County friends who are hard at work in the garden. Look carefully at their faces. Color one critter who is practicing what the verse means. Then say the verse again. Color another critter who is obeying God's Word.

Let's Talk About It:

• What are some of the jobs you have to do to help your family?

• Do you like to work hard? Why or why not?

Let's Pray About It:

There are times when everyone has trouble wanting to do a job right. When you pray today, ask Jesus to help you do your best work even when you don't feel like it.

Memory Verse: Whatever you do, work at it with all your heart. Colossians 3:23a (NIV)

Day 9 • Monday

L ook at Glitter and Sparkle. Which one is about to plug in the beautiful lights? It looks like they're getting ready for Christmas, doesn't it? But look again. See the words printed on the branches? This is a fruit tree—a "fruit of the Spirit" tree. When we are Jesus' children, the Spirit of God lights up our lives with love, joy, and other good things. Color this picture to make it beautiful. How many lights can you see on the tree? _____
Listen as your mom or dad reads the "fruit of the Spirit" words and explains words you don't understand.

Let's Talk About It:

• When do you feel close to God? Do you feel close to him 24 hours a day, 7 days a week? Do you think he is always with you?

• Can you see any "fruit of the Spirit" in your life? Ask what good thing your mom or dad sees in your life.

Let's Pray About It:

When you pray today, ask Jesus to use a good thing in your life to make someone else happy.

Memory Verse: Whatever you do, work at it with all your heart. Colossians 3:23a (NIV)

Day 10 • Tuesday

P O W E R

p r a y

b i b l e

T he Power Buddies are having a hard time figuring out what words these pictures stand for. They want to be like Jesus 24 hours a day, 7 days a week. Can you help them? Figure out each word by writing the first letter of each picture on the line below it.

Let's Talk About It:

• How does prayer power us up? How many times a week do you pray?

• The Bible also helps to power us up. What Bible story have you read or heard this week?

Let's Pray About It:

When you pray today, ask Jesus to help you power up with prayer and Bible reading.

Memory Verse: Whatever you do, work at it with all your heart. Colossians 3:23a (NIV)

ANSWERS: power, pray, Bible

Day 11 • Wednesday

L ook at Lester. He sure has learned this week memory's verse, hasn't he? He is working with his whole heart—and a lot of sweat!!

Can you help him get his car up the hill? It would really help him push better if you would connect the dots. Start with number 1, then draw a line to number 2. Keep going until you've connected all the dots. . . . Work with all your heart.

Let's Talk About It:

• What kinds of work do you like to do? What jobs don't you like?

• Why do you think God wants us to do our work with all our heart?

Let's Pray About It:

When you pray today, ask Jesus to help you do your hard jobs well. And then be sure to remember to thank him when he answers you.

Memory Verse: Whatever you do, work at it with all your heart. Colossians 3:23a (NIV)

Day 12 • Thursday

T he pictures the critters are holding up are meant to help you think of things people pray for. Color the pictures that remind you of something you have prayed about. Jesus hears our prayers 24 hours a day, 7 days a week. He has promised to give us the things we need, but not everything we want. Sometimes the things we think we need and want would really be bad for us. When we ask Jesus for things like that, he will tell us no.

Let's Talk About It:

• Has Jesus ever told you no when you asked him for something? What did he say no to?

• Has Jesus ever told you yes when you asked him for something? What did he say yes to?

Let's Pray About It:

Think of something to pray about that is very important to you. Then use your own words to make a prayer about it. Give it your best effort. Tell Jesus how you feel and how you would like for him to answer.

Memory Verse: Whatever you do, work at it with all your heart. Colossians 3:23a (NIV)

Day 13 • Friday

E verything changes. Only God stays the same. Look at the pictures at the top. Each of these will change into one of the people or animals at the bottom. Draw a line from the person or animal above to what he or she will become.

You will change too. Your age changes each year. One day you will become a man or woman. But if you believe in Jesus, one thing will never change: You will always be his child.

Let's Talk About It:

• What are some other things that change? (For example, the seasons.) What are some things that don't change? (For example, Christmas is always December 25.)

• How do you feel knowing that God never changes?

Let's Pray About It:

When you pray today, ask Jesus to help you be more like him each day. He will help you say and do the right things.

Memory Verse: Whatever you do, work at it with all your heart. Colossians 3:23a (NIV)

Days 14 and 15 • Saturday and Sunday

W hen our family and friends touch us with their love, it makes us feel happy! When we are loved, we have the power to share our love with others. And when we show love to others, those people will show love to others too. All this love sure puts a big smile on Jesus' face!

Read today's memory verse, then color one of the children. Try to say the verse from memory, then color the other child. After that, say the verse a third time, and make Glitter sparkle. Say it one more time, and make Sparkle glitter.

Let's Talk About It:

• When was the last time you felt sad? Did somebody help you feel better? How?

• What does it mean to you when someone gives you hug or a kiss?

Let's Pray About It:

When you pray today, ask Jesus to help you show people that you love them. And ask him to help you see who needs a kind word or a loving hug.

Memory Verse: Above all, love each other deeply. 1 Peter 4:8a (NIV)

Day 16 • Monday

L iona Lou says it's party time in Critter County! She's about to share some of her homemade goodies with her friends. This is her way of saying, "Welcome! Glad you're here!" Sharing good things always puts a smile on the faces of our friends. Can you count how many cupcakes she has on her tray? Count out loud. How many cups does she have? How many balloons are in the room? Count out loud.

Can you guess why she's having a party? Maybe she's celebrating something that happened to Sydney. Why don't you read the story "Sydney Learns to Share" to find out more about it? The story begins on page 7.

Let's Talk About It:

• Is it ever hard for you to share with other kids? Why is that?

• Why do you think God want us to learn to share?

Let's Pray About It:

Dear Jesus, help me to want to share with others. Thank you for what you have given me. Amen.

Memory Verse: Above all, love each other deeply. 1 Peter 4:8a (NIV)

Day 17 • Tuesday

H ave you ever played soccer? Would you like to play with your friends in Critter County? See how happy they look. They enjoy being together because they take care of each other. Can you find some critters in this picture who are sharing something? Show them that you're proud of them by coloring them as nicely as you can.

Let's Talk About It:

• When we are kind and we share, who is pleased about it?

• What are some ways you can be kind?

Let's Pray About It:

When you pray today, ask Jesus to help power you up with a loving attitude toward others. This will make sharing with others easier.

Memory Verse: Above all, love each other deeply. 1 Peter 4:8a (NIV)

Power Booster
Memory Verses

1. We know that in all things God works for the good of those who love him.

Romans 8:28a (NIV)

2. Whatever you do, work at it with all your heart.

Colossians 3:23a (NIV)

3. Above all, love each other deeply.

1 Peter 4:8a (NIV)

4. We will speak the truth with love.

Ephesians 4:15a (ICB)

5. Our Father in heaven,
hallowed be your name.

Matthew 6:9 (NIV)

6. Give thanks to the Lord. . . .
Tell about all the wonderful
things he has done.

Psalm 105:1-2 (ICB)

7. Let peace hold
you together.

Ephesians 4:3b (ICB)

8. I want to know Christ.

Philippians 3:10a (NIV)

Day 18 • Wednesday

T ake a good look at these pictures. No, you're not seeing double! Or are you? In both pictures, Sydney is about to welcome guests into his home. But there are seven things missing in the second picture that are in the first picture. Can you find them all?

Let's Talk About It:

• Who would you like to invite to your home to play? Who do you like to play with at school?

• What would you like to share with this friend?

Let's Pray About It:

When you pray today, ask Jesus to help you be a good host. That means you will make your guests feel welcome by sharing your things with them.

Memory Verse: Above all, love each other deeply. 1 Peter 4:8a (NIV)

Day 19 • Thursday

A sk your mom or dad to help you think of five good things you can do today that will show someone else you love him or her. Maybe you can share something with your brother or sister, or help feed your pet. Every time you do something, put a check mark in one of the boxes on the chart that Glitter and Sparkle are holding. How long do you think it will take you to fill up the chart?

Let's Talk About It:

• How do you feel inside when you do something good for someone else? Why is that?

• Can you say this week's memory verse and tell someone what it means?

Let's Pray About It:

It sure is easy just to think about ourselves and what we want, isn't it? So when you pray today, ask Jesus to continue to help you become a power sharer. A power sharer is a kid who has learned to be loving and kind.

Memory Verse: Above all, love each other deeply. 1 Peter 4:8a (NIV)

Day 20 • Friday

S ome of our Critter County friends remember what this week's memory verse is all about, while others have forgotten it. Can you say or read the verse out loud to them? Then color in the kids and critters who have chosen to obey God. Don't color the kids and critters who forgot. They need to stay in black and white until they learn to behave, don't they?

Let's Talk About It:

• Can you think of a time when you didn't behave in a loving way? How did you feel inside?

• How can you set things right when you disobey God?

Let's Pray About It:

Dear Jesus, show me how to be loving and kind to someone today. Amen.

Memory Verse: Above all, love each other deeply. 1 Peter 4:8a (NIV)

Days 21 and 22 • Saturday and Sunday

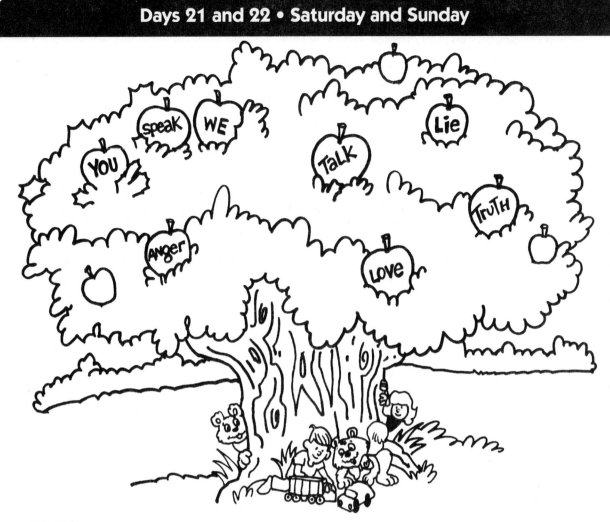

T oday we begin Week 4 of our Adventure. That means we will start to work on a new memory verse. The tree above has some of the words from the verse written on the fruit. It also has some wrong words hanging on it. Read the new verse three times. Then cover it with your hand or a strip of paper. Circle the words in the tree that are part of the verse. Cross out the words that aren't part of the verse. Uncover the verse to see if you got it right. You can ask a parent for help if you need to.

Let's Talk About It:

• What does it mean to "speak the truth"?

• Who do you think wants you to "speak the truth"?

Let's Pray About It:

Have you ever been tempted to lie to keep out of trouble or to get what you wanted? If so, you're not alone. But lying is wrong. When you pray today, ask God to help you be truthful, even when it's hard to do.

Memory Verse: We will speak the truth with love. Ephesians 4:15a (ICB)

Day 23 • Monday

1	Blue
2	Red
3	Yellow
4	Brown
5	Purple

H ow does it make you feel when someone says to you "Way to go!" or "Great job!"? Pretty good, right? Your church school teacher and all the people who lead your church are just like you. It makes them feel good to know that they are doing their jobs well. Have you ever told any of them the truth about how much you have learned from them? Have you ever thanked Jesus for them?

The folks of Critter County love their church and Pastor Penguin. Just look at how they are letting him know. Color this happy scene. There's a color key to help you get the stained glass window just right.

Let's Talk About It:

• What do you like most about your pastor or church school teacher?

• What could you do this week to let your pastor or teacher know you care?

Let's Pray About It:

When you pray today, ask Jesus to give your teacher and pastor lots of energy and power so they can keep on helping more people like you.

Memory Verse: We will speak the truth with love. Ephesians 4:15a (ICB)

Day 24 • Tuesday

W hen we go to church, we grow stronger in spirit because we find both love and God's truth there. These sad critters could use a bit of God's love and truth, don't you agree? How about helping them find their way to church? Then help them find their way back home again.

Let's Talk About It:

• What do you like best about your church?

• How do your church leaders help you and your family?

Let's Pray About It:

Are there any special needs at your church that you know about? Is someone sick or in need of a job? Is the church looking for a new pastor or youth worker? When you pray today, include these needs. Children's prayers can be powerful!

Memory Verse: We will speak the truth with love. Ephesians 4:15a (ICB)

Day 25 • Wednesday

H ave you ever noticed how a big hug can power you up when you're feeling down? Glitter needed a hug, and her church school teacher was happy to give her one. Just connect the dots by following the numbers to help her teacher make Glitter feel better. Start with the number 1 and connect the dots. When you are finished, you will see how much better Glitter feels after a hug from her teacher.

Let's Talk About It:

• Who gives you the hugs you need?

• Who have you cheered up lately? Have you cheered up a grown-up? How?

Let's Pray About It:

Dear Jesus, I want to cheer up people and love others. Show me someone to hug today. Amen.

Memory Verse: We will speak the truth with love. Ephesians 4:15a (ICB)

Day 26 • Thursday

D o you like to get mail? It's fun, isn't it? Grown-ups like to get mail too. That's why the Power Buddies are writing a note to their church school teacher. They know they can give their teacher a power boost with a few kind words. How about you? Would you be willing to write a note or draw a nice picture for your church school teacher? You don't have to be a firefly to be a Power Buddy to someone else.

Let's Talk About It:

• What does a kind, loving voice sound like? Can you sound loving and kind?

• Can you think of something you could say to help someone feel better?

Let's Pray About It:

When you pray today, remember to pray for any people in your family, church, or neighborhood who may need love or kindness right now.

Memory Verse: We will speak the truth with love. Ephesians 4:15a (ICB)

Day 27 • Friday

C an you guess why this teacher looks so happy? Do you think it has anything to do with the way the kids are paying attention and trying to answer the questions? Yes, you're right. That's it exactly. It's fun to teach a class of kids who are excited about learning. Do you ever put a smile on your teacher's face this way?

To help you remember how important it is to make your teacher smile, Sydney wants you to color his teacher's face. Then he says for you to have fun looking for other things in the picture that start with the letter "S." Color them, too. How many did you find? _____

Let's Talk About It:

• Think of a time your teacher was really happy. What was going on in class?

• Do you ever ask questions in your class? Can you think of a question about Jesus that you would like to ask your teacher or pastor?

Let's Pray About It:

When you pray today, remember to pray for your teacher and the kids in your class. Ask Jesus to help the children to be good listeners and workers. And ask him to help your teacher make learning fun for everyone.

Memory Verse: We will speak the truth with love. Ephesians 4:15a (ICB)

Days 28 and 29 • Saturday and Sunday

I n this week's new verse, there's a big word that you probably don't know. It's the word *hallowed*. It means to honor or show respect. So when you tell God that his name should be hallowed, you are saying that he should be honored or praised. Look at Sydney's list of words above. Circle the ones that could be used to honor God. (Ask a grown-up to help you with the words you may not know.)

Let's Talk About It:

• Which of the words on Sydney's list do you think fit God best?

• Why should we honor God?

Let's Pray About It:

When you pray today, choose your favorite words from Sydney's list and use them to honor God.

Memory Verse: Our Father in heaven, hallowed be your name. Matthew 6:9 (NIV)

Day 30 • Monday

D o you know someone who deserves some special attention or honor? How about making this person an award badge? All you need to make it is a sheet of white paper, a pencil, some crayons, and a pair of scissors. You can even make more than one badge, if you like. Just place the paper on top of the badge pattern above, and trace the lines. Write a message on the badge, then color and cut it out.

Let's Talk About It:

• How else could you honor someone besides giving him or her a badge?

• Who are some of the people in your church who deserve to be honored?

Let's Pray About It:

When you pray today, tell Jesus about the people you would like to honor. Thank him for bringing them into your life.

Memory Verse: Our Father in heaven, hallowed be your name. Matthew 6:9 (NIV)

Day 31 • Tuesday

Dear Jesus,

Fruit is good for you.

Amen.

Thank you for my family.

Thank you that I am your child.

Dogs and cats fight sometimes.

H ave you ever written a prayer to Jesus? Would you like to try it? Look at the words above. Circle the ones you might use if you were praying to him. Then try writing your own prayer on the lines. Or, say your prayer to someone. Thank Jesus for making the things in the world that you enjoy and for making you.

Let's Talk About It:

• Jesus loves it when we read about him, sing about him, or pray to him. Which do you like to do best?

• In what kind of books do you read about Jesus?

Let's Pray About It:

Use the prayer that you wrote today to show Jesus honor. Then sing a song about him.

Memory Verse: Our Father in heaven, hallowed be your name. Matthew 6:9 (NIV)

Day 32 • Wednesday

prayer, fighting, helping Mom, being kind, making a mess, working on my 50-Day Adventure book

J esus spent a lot of time talking to his Father in prayer. He also spent a lot of time helping people.

Can you tell time? Do you have your own clock or watch? Clocks and watches help us keep track of time. It's up to us to make good use of our time. Add the missing numbers to the face of the clock above. Then circle the words that tell about good ways to use time.

Let's Talk About It:

• What do you spend most of your time doing each day?

• Do you think this is a wise use of your time? What do your parents think?

Let's Pray About It:

When you pray today, ask Jesus to help you learn to use your time wisely. Time is one thing we can't get back. When it's gone, it's gone forever. So we need to use our time to do the things that are most important to us and to Jesus.

Memory Verse: Our Father in heaven, hallowed be your name. Matthew 6:9 (NIV)

Day 33 • Thursday

D o you enjoy going to church to pray with your family and friends? As you can see, the folks of Critter County love to get together to worship and honor Jesus. How about adding your own picture to this scene? There's room for you. When you've finished drawing your own picture, write your name in the box. Wouldn't it be fun to really be there with all your critter friends?

Let's Talk About It:

• What is your favorite song about Jesus? Which Critter County memory verse song do like best so far? Why?

• Which Critter County friend do you like best? How do you think it would sound if this critter sang your favorite song?

Let's Pray About It:

When you pray today, thank Jesus for your church family, and sing him your favorite song. He'll be sure to love it.

Memory Verse: Our Father in heaven, hallowed be your name. Matthew 6:9 (NIV)

Day 34 • Friday

O ne of the critters' friends has looked and looked all over for her missing Bible. Can you find it? Please circle it. It's time to for her to pray and work on her 50-Day Adventure book. After you find the Bible, color the whole picture with happy, bright colors. She and the critters will really appreciate your help.

Let's Talk About It:

• Where do you keep your Bible so it won't get lost?

• When do you pray each day?

Let's Pray About It:

Dear Jesus, thank you for giving us your Word, the Bible. Thank you for always having time to hear my prayers. Amen.

Memory Verse: Our Father in heaven, hallowed be your name. Matthew 6:9 (NIV)

Days 35 and 36 • Saturday and Sunday

I t's Week 6 of the Adventure! Time for another new memory verse. Read the verse six times. Each time you read it, write or draw a gift God has given you on one of the blank lines. For example, if you're glad God gave you a family, draw their picture or write "my family" on one of the blank lines. If you can think of more than six gifts God has given you, write or draw these, too. (Use any space on the page you can find.)

Just look at all the ways God has shown you he loves you! Isn't it wonderful?

Let's Talk About It:

• Ask your parents to tell you about some of the gifts has God given them.

• What kinds of gifts does God want from us?

Let's Pray About It:

When you pray today, thank Jesus for every gift you put on your list. And ask him to help you tell other people about him.

Memory Verse: Give thanks to the Lord. . . . Tell about all the wonderful things he has done. Psalm 105:1-2 (ICB)

Day 37 • Monday

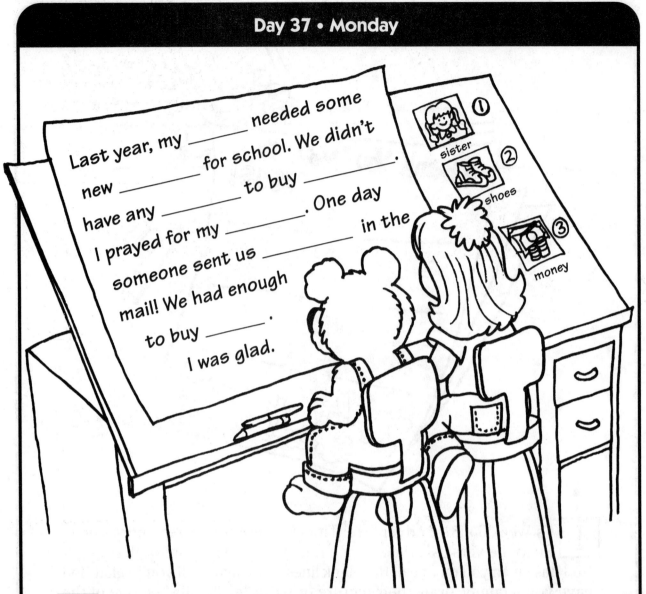

Last year, my _____ needed some new _____ for school. We didn't have any _____ to buy _____. I prayed for my _____. One day someone sent us _____ in the mail! We had enough to buy _____. I was glad.

① sister
② shoes
③ money

L unchbox wants to help a friend write a story about how God helped her sister. You can help them by choosing the person or thing that will fill each blank space in the story. Write the number of the picture that should go in each space.

Let's Talk About It:

• Who have you helped lately? What did you do?

• Have you told somebody about Jesus? That's one way to help someone!

Let's Pray About It:

When you pray the Son Power Prayer, thank Jesus for being your helper. Then ask him to help you tell somebody about him.

Memory Verse: Give thanks to the Lord. . . . Tell about all the wonderful things he has done. Psalm 105:1-2 (ICB)

Day 38 • Tuesday

J esus told a lot of stories. He wanted people to understand how much his Father loved them. See if you can put this story that Jesus told in order. Do you know it? It is the story of how Jesus fed over 5,000 people. Glitter wants you to go for it! Number the pictures 1, 2, or 3 to show what happened first, second, and third.

Let's Talk About It:

• Do you know the whole story of the Prodigal Son?

• Who first told you about God?

Let's Pray About It:

Tell Jesus thanks for the person who first told you about him.

Memory Verse: Give thanks to the Lord. . . . Tell about all the wonderful things he has done. Psalm 105:1-2 (ICB)

Day 39 • Wednesday

L unchbox is learning to read, just like you, but he still enjoys being read to. One of his favorite books is a Bible storybook his grandma gave him. He likes the story of Noah best. What is your favorite Bible story? Write the name of the story on the front of the book above. Then draw a picture from the story on a piece of drawing paper.

Let's Talk About It:

• Who tells you Bible stories? Who reads you Bible stories? Which story do you like best?

• Have you ever told or read someone a Bible story? Who was it?

Let's Pray About It:

When you pray today, ask Jesus to help you learn more about the Bible so that you can tell other people about it. Then give the Bible-story picture you drew to a friend. If your friend asks you what the picture is about, offer to tell him or her the whole story.

Memory Verse: Give thanks to the Lord. . . . Tell about all the wonderful things he has done. Psalm 105:1-2 (ICB)

Day 40 • Thursday

P oor Lester. He has a special project to make for his church school class. But he can't find the tools he needs. Can you help him find his hammer, screwdriver, saw and two nails? Thanks! This will really help him out. He wants to give each child and critter in his class a small wooden cross for Easter.

Let's Talk About It:

• What Bible story does a cross make you think of?

• If Jesus died on a cross, why are we happy at Eastertime?

Let's Pray About It:

After you pray the Son Power Prayer today (p. 2), sing the song "Wonderful Things" if you know it. Then thank Jesus for all the wonderful things he has done, like dying for us on the cross.

Memory Verse: Give thanks to the Lord. . . . Tell about all the wonderful things he has done. Psalm 105:1-2 (ICB)

Day 41 • Friday

The Power Buddies are cheering, "Go team! Go!" The Critter County basketball team is playing its last game of the season. Everyone is so excited. If they win, they get the trophy. And they'll get their names and pictures in the newspaper, too. The good news will travel fast and far!

Think of a cheer to tell Jesus something you like about him. Call out your cheer loud and long. And jump up and down, too, if you feel like it.

Let's Talk About It:

• Can you make up a cheer using this week's memory verse? Try it!

• How can we spread the good news about Jesus to the whole world?

Let's Pray About It:

When you pray today, thank Jesus for making it possible for you to learn about him. And ask him to help you get excited about telling others about him too.

Memory Verse: Give thanks to the Lord. . . . Tell about all the wonderful things he has done. Psalm 105:1-2 (ICB)

Days 42 and 43 • Saturday and Sunday

L ook at how happy these puppies are. They are happy because they are with their mommy. It looks like they've learned this week's memory verse. Read the verse one time. Then count how many spots you can see on the mother dog. Hold up your fingers to show the answer. Read the verse again and count how many spots you see on each puppy. Hold up your fingers to show each answer.

Hey, wait a minute. Who is the visitor at this meal? She seems to be enjoying herself. Read the verse again. Then count how many stripes she has. Hold up your fingers to show the answer.

Let's Talk About It:

• What does the word *peace* mean? Ask your mom or dad to help you understand that word.

• What are some good ways to make peace with your friends and family?

Let's Pray About It:

When you pray today, thank Jesus for everyone who loves you and brings peace into your life.

Memory Verse: Let peace hold you together. Ephesians 4:3b (ICB)

Day 44 • Monday

H ave you ever gone camping? Doesn't it look like the critters are having a good time together? You can learn more about this camping trip by turning back to page 12 and reading the story "Critters to the Rescue." Then turn back here and color this peaceful scene.

Let's Talk About It:

• What did each critter do to help rescue Lunchbox? Did they work together well?

• Name all the different feelings Lunchbox felt during this camping trip. Did he ever get angry? Why not?

Let's Pray About It:

Dear Jesus, help me stay calm and peaceful when trouble comes. Show me what I can do to help others. Amen.

Memory Verse: Let peace hold you together. Ephesians 4:3b (ICB)

Day 45 • Tuesday

L ook at the pictures above very carefully. Put an X across the ones that show pictures of kids and critters who are forgetting to obey this week's Bible verse. Then color the pictures of the kids and critters who are playing and working together peacefully.

Let's Talk About It:

• Which of your friends do you enjoy being with the most? Why is that?

• Who do you have trouble getting along with? Why is that?

Let's Pray About It:

When you pray today, ask Jesus to help you learn to live in peace with everyone you possibly can. And ask him to help you learn how to make up when someone gets angry with you.

Memory Verse: Let peace hold you together. Ephesians 4:3b (ICB)

Day 46 • Wednesday

L ester and Liona Lou want to help Sydney pack a picnic basket for the church picnic. See if you can help them pack the basket. What should go in it? Circle the things you think should go in his basket. Or, you and your family can take turns calling out the things that should go in the basket.

Let's Talk About It:

• What teams have you been a part of? Did they work together well?

• Why do you think God wants his people to worship together instead of alone?

Let's Pray About It:

When you pray today, thank God for giving you a church family to worship with. Thank him for each of the kids in your church school class.

Memory Verse: Let peace hold you together. Ephesians 4:3b (ICB)

Day 47 • Thursday

One of the easiest and best ways we can work to keep things peaceful is to pray for the people we know. Can you think of someone who could use a loving prayer right now? Are any of your friends or family members sick or sad or having a hard time? Pray for them. It's a great way to show them you care. Then let them know about it by sending them a note like the Power Buddies are sending to Lester.

Let's Talk About It:

• If you had a problem, would it help you to know that someone was praying for you? Why?

• Have you ever prayed with someone else about a problem? Did praying together feel more powerful than praying alone?

Let's Pray About It:

When you pray today, pray with your whole family, if possible. Thank God for showing us how to live in peace with each other.

Memory Verse: Let peace hold you together. Ephesians 4:3b (ICB)

Day 48 • Friday

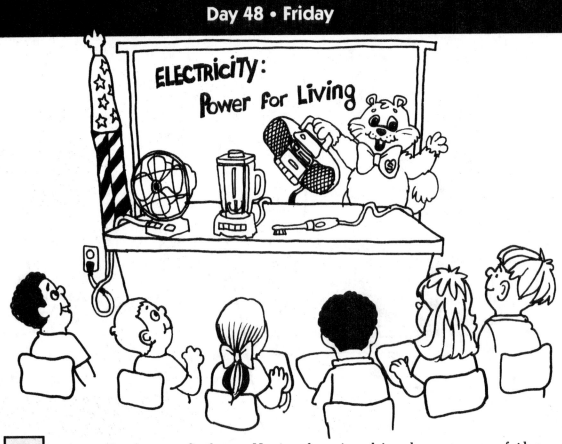

L ook at Professor Sydney. He is showing his class some of the wonderful things electrical power can do. How many things can you find in this picture that use electrical power? _____ What would happen if these things were unplugged? Why?

Do all electrical appliances have cords? If not, how do they get their power? What do you have to put inside them to get them to work?

Prayer helps us "plug in" to God's power line. When we pray, he fills us with his love and peace. And memorizing God's Word, the Bible, is like putting a battery full of God's power inside us. We can take this Son Power with us wherever we go. It can last a lifetime.

Let's Talk About It:

• Celebrating Son Power means telling Jesus how glad you are that he helps you. What do you know about Jesus that makes you like him?

• What would you tell a friend about Jesus?

Let's Pray About It:

When you pray today, tell Jesus that you want to know him better. Ask him to help you become a better listener in church school and church.

Memory Verse: I want to know Christ. Philippians 3:10a (NIV)

Day 49 • Saturday

G|randma Lulu Lioness was very old when she died. Her family misses her, but they aren't sad anymore because they know she is with Jesus in heaven. They know she is very happy there.

Lunchbox thinks heaven is like a big park with grassy fields to run and play in. Liona Lou thinks of heaven as a beautiful garden full of flowers. Lester thinks of heaven as a place where everyone is strong and healthy. But they all agree that what will make heaven a gr-r-r-eat place to live someday is that they'll get to be with Jesus—and with Grandma Lulu.

Let's Talk About It:

• Why is it that we can be sad and happy when someone we love goes to heaven?

• What do think heaven will be like?

Let's Pray About It:

When you pray today, thank Jesus for making it possible for us to go to heaven when we die. And thank him for showing us that we don't have to be afraid of the future. He is with us now, and he will be with us always.

Memory Verse: I want to know Christ. Philippians 3:10a (NIV)

Day 50 • Sunday

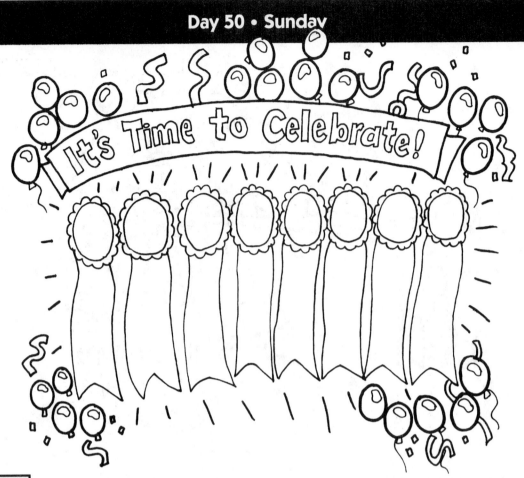

Y ou did it! You made it all the way through this 50-Day Adventure! Now that's something to celebrate! Sydney, the Power Buddies, the Lion Family, and your family are all very proud of you. Can you say each of the eight Adventure memory verses? Give it a try. Each time you get one right, color an award ribbon blue.

Can you think of some other reasons to celebrate today? How about celebrating the Good News of Jesus' resurrection? (That's a big word meaning he came back to life after dying on the cross.) Color the picture above with happy colors to show you agree that this is good news.

Let's Talk About It:

• What did you like the most about this Adventure?

• What did you learn that you didn't know before?

Let's Pray About It:

When you pray today, thank Jesus for all the answers to prayer that he has given you during this Adventure. And tell him that you want to keep on talking with him because he is your special friend.

Memory Verse: I want to know Christ. Philippians 3:10a (NIV)

D raw a picture of yourself in the frame that Sydney is holding. On the lines under the frame, write a few words that tell what's special about you. Then have your mom or dad fill out the form on the next page. Send it to the Critter County Post Office in care of Mainstay Church Resources. The critters will send you a tape called *Heroes Come in All Sizes*. You'll love the fun songs and special story about Sydney, Lester, Liona Lou, Lunchbox, and lots more Critter County friends!

Please Send Us Your Free Critter County Audiotape, *Heroes Come in All Sizes!*

Child's Name _____ Age _____

Parent's Name _____

Street Address* _____

City_____State/Prov _____ Zip/Code _____

*Note: UPS will not deliver to a P. O. box.

Please Send the Following Additional Critter County Products:

Item	Title	Price	Quantity	Total
451K	***Critter County Power Buddies*** Children's Stories & Bible Songs Audiotape $6.00		_____	_____
8431	***Rack, Shack, and Benny*** VeggieTales® Videotape $15.00		_____	_____
2740	***Critter County Clubhouse*** Children's Activity Book $6.00		_____	_____
450X	***Critter County Clubhouse*** Children's Scripture Memory Audiotape $6.00		_____	_____
2640	***Pack Up My Backpack*** Children's Activity Book $6.00		_____	_____
450S	***Pack Up My Backpack*** Children's Scripture Memory Audiotape $6.00		_____	_____
2540	***Facing the Fearigators*** Children's Activity Book $6.00		_____	_____
450A	***Beating the Fearigators*** Children's Scripture Memory Audiotape $6.00		_____	_____

Subtotal	**$**	
Add 10% for UPS shipping/handling ($4.00 minimum)	**$**	_____
Canadian or Illinois residents add 7% GST/sales tax.	**$**	_____
Total (subtotal + shipping + tax)	**$**	
Total Amount Enclosed	**$**	

Mail this order form (with your check, if you're ordering other products) to:

Mainstay Church Resources, Box 30, Wheaton, IL 60189-0030

In Canada: The Chapel Ministries, Box 2000, Waterdown, ON L0R 2H0

For VISA, MasterCard, or Discover card orders call 1-800-224-2735 (U.S.) or 1-800-461-4114 (Canada).

MO7CCJ98